PREVAILING PRAYERS FOR

FIRST BORN

AND

DESTINY RECOVERY PRAYERS

HELEN AYENI

PREVAILING PRAYERS FOR FIRST BORN

Website: www.gloriousmwo.org
Email: gloriousmwo@gmail.com
Phone # 972-348-8270

Printed in the United States of America.
First Printing 2024
Published By:

Vision Power Publishers
P. O Box 2611,
Arlington TX. 76004
www.visionpowerpublishers.com

Content Guide

Chapter

Forward

It is my great pleasure to share with you ***"Prevailing Prayers For First Born,"*** a book dedicated to all the firstborns in our families. There is no doubt that being the first isn't always easy, but it is also an amazing honor.

I believe that every firstborn deserves to be celebrated and prayed for. This book contains heartfelt prayers and blessings that are intended to uplift and encourage those who hold the honor of being the firstborn in their family.

This book delves into the depths of a mother's heart as she calls on God for protection over her child. You'll feel the raw emotions that come with being a parent - the joys, fears, hopes, and dreams. The words in this book, ***"Prevailing Prayers for First Born"*** are not merely ink on paper. They hold a deeper meaning.

They serve as a guide for navigating the difficult moments of life with strength and faith, through the power of prayer. No matter what obstacles you may face or how confusing the world may seem, this book can provide comfort and motivation to keep pushing forward.

Joshua 1:9 states, ***"Be strong and of good courage; do not be afraid, nor be dismayed, for the Lord your God is with you wherever you go."*** This verse serves as a reminder that even when we feel lost or unsure, God remains by our side, providing us with the necessary strength and courage we need to persevere.

Let this book serve as a source of hope and inspiration as you navigate the challenges of life. Turn to prayer, seek guidance from God, and trust that He will lead you towards a brighter tomorrow.

As stated in Proverbs 3:6, ***"In all your ways acknowledge Him, and He shall direct your paths."***

I can't wait for you to start reading!

Benjamin Beckley
The Empowerment Center

Dedication

With gratitude to the Almighty God, who is worthy to be praised, I humbly dedicate this book to my parents, **Pastor Michael and Pastor Mrs. Elizabeth Siyaka.** They are so lovely, nurturing, caring, warm-hearted, and lovers of God. My parents constant prayers were the reason for my divine encounter with God. Both of you will forever be remembered for your good work.

Acknowledgment

I acknowledge our God, the everlasting God, who has preserved my life from death and danger. If it were not for the Lord, I would not be alive to write this book. All praises and adoration go to you.

I would like to acknowledge my parents, Pastor and Pastor Mrs. Siyaka, who are always fasting and praying for their children to be closer to God. You are both loved and appreciated.

I would like to express my heartfelt gratitude to my beloved husband, Pastor Layo Ayeni, and my wonderful children for their unwavering love and unrelenting support.

I am truly grateful to my mentor, Pastor James and his wife Dcns. Tomi Olaleye. Your presence in our ministry has been a tremendous blessing to all of us. Thank you for your guidance and support.

I want to express my gratitude to Pastor Benjamin and Pastor Mrs. Beckley of the Empowerment Center for inspiring me to write this book.

Your encouragement means so much to me, and I pray that God will abundantly bless you for your kindness. Thank you for being a beacon of light in my life!

I also want to express my appreciation and gratitude to Pastor Christopher and his wife, Pastor Mrs. Jumoke Adetoro and the entire membership of RCCG, Bread of Life for their genuine love and unconditional support.

I am immensely grateful to sister Francisca Aisebonaye for the time you took to edit the manuscript and also to the ***Glorious Ministries' World Outreach*** partners and their unwavering support. Every one of you shall be scaling new heights

Also, thanks be to Pastor Bola Adejagun for her constant prayers and advice. May you continue to wax strong and stronger. I cannot but also appreciate Pastor Musa Idris and his loving wife, Mrs. Christy Musa for being supportive at all times.

I appreciate every pastors who have prayed and assisted me in the ministry. None of you shall lack destiny helpers in Jesus name Amen.

Finally, I am truly grateful to my siblings, Pastor Victoria, the founder of Tabernacle Praise Church, Minister Francis, and Pastor Emmanuel the founder of Favored Church, and Christopher. You all mean so much to me, and I want you to know how much I love each and every one of you. Thank you!

Introduction

This is the first edition of my prayer book for firstborns, and it also includes special prayers that are tailored to help you with your own spiritual journey, including specific prayers designed to address personal spiritual challenges.

It is imperative to take proactive measures to safeguard your child's future from potential threats. Therefore, it is crucial to take a stand and fight against any adversaries. With divine assistance, one can exercise authority over the influence of Satan. As stated in the Bible: ***"I give you authority over all the power of the enemy."*** (Luke 10:19)

Through intercessory prayer, you can protect your firstborn or children from evil forces and negative influences. Your prayers have the power to bring blessings and success to them in the present and future. While utilizing this book, try and quote the Bible scriptures, fast, live a pure life, sow a seed on behalf of your first born and teach them the word of God.

Please share your testimonies as God gives your firstborn victory over the power of darkness.

I pray that every concern of your life will be turned towards the order of good news and testimony.

After using this book to pray, may the Lord open a new chapter for your firstborn. ***"Thou said the Lord as the new wine is found in the cluster and one saith destroy it not; for there is a blessing in it, so shall I do for my servant sake, that I might not destroy it all"*** (Isaiah 65:8). Therefore, there is a blessing in your firstborn and no evil shall befall him or her. I declare that the journey of your firstborn will keep getting brighter and better in all aspects of his or her existence. Amen!

Contact:
Evang. Helen Ayeni
Glorious Ministries' World Outreach
Gministrymwo@gmail.com
972-348-8270
www.gloriousmwo.org

Nigeria Bank Account
Saving Acct:0089783561
Name of Bank: Sterling Bank

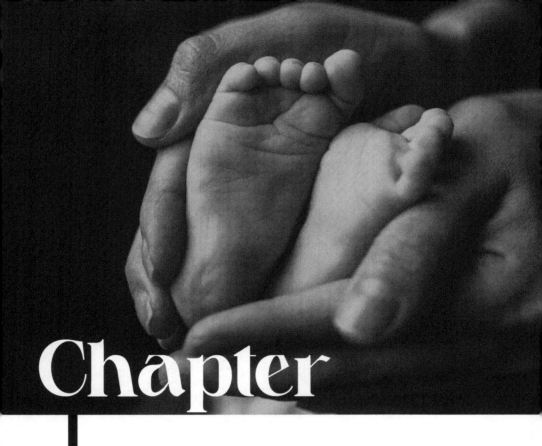

Chapter

1

WHY WE NEED TO SANCTIFY OUR FIRSTBORN

Why we need to sanctify our firstborn

"And the LORD spake unto Moses, saying, Sanctify unto me all the firstborn, whatsoever openeth the womb among the children of Israel, both of and of beast: it is mine"
(Exodus 13:1-2)

Sanctification is an act of declaring something Holy. The Lord admonished us through the above scripture why we need to take responsibility by training our children in the way of the Lord and the importance of dedicating them for God use and his glory. Paying attention to first child's spiritual journey is very important the Bible records it, that we should train our children in the way of the Lord and he will not depart from it. (Proverb 22:6).

If we sanctify our first born to God, that means, God is the caretaker of the child and the purpose of that child fulfilling destiny is certain.

There are basics principles to be taken to live a life of purpose.

- Inform your firstborn their important role with their stand in the Lord.
- Teach your first born the right road map to their destiny through God's word.
- Spend time with your firstborn by teaching them life experience that would make them understand the concepts of life.
- Start a dialogue with your firstborn to explain the insights of staying Holy to accomplish divine purpose

TWO PRACTICAL METHODS TO HELP FIRST BORN

1. Mentorship

First born are very important to God, as a result the enemy will want to destroy the relationship between the first born and God. Therefore, it is very imperative that first born are protected from sin and when the baby is born the parents needs to mentor the child by teaching him or her the word of God based on this scripture.

"This book of the law shall not depart out of thy mouth; but thou shalt meditate therein day and night, that thou mayest observe to do according to all that is written therein: for then thou shalt make thy way prosperous, and then thou shalt have good success. (Joshua 1:8).

2. Dedication

For this child I prayed; and the LORD hath given me my petition which I asked of him: Therefore also I have lent him to the LORD; as long as he liveth he shall be lent to the LORD. And he worshiped the LORD there. (1 Samuel:27-28).

Hannah made a vow to the altar of God by dedicating a child which has not be born. In turn, the child became the ownership to the almighty God. That is why when Samuel was born his life style followed God's plan due to the vow of dedication. If an unbeliever dedicate his or her first born to herbalist, that child will begin to misbehave. When parents make a godly vow on behalf of a born or unborn child that means the parents indicate to raise the child according to the instruction of the Holy Spirit, by praying, teaching, training and disciplining the child in the way of God.

ANOTHER CONSIDERATION FOR FIRST BORN IS THE SOURCE OF FOUNDATION

There is a lot of great joy and expectation when a mother is about to deliver her first born. As, the mother and the father are joyful, if the foundation of the parents are faulty, the foundation of the parents can affect the destiny of their firstborn. What is foundation? Foundation is the genesis or the root of what happened at the beginning of your life. It is also what your ancestors or your parents have put together or prepared during their existence whether good or bad.

Your character or traits can also be inherited through your blood line .Foundation also simply means what happened to you during the moment when you were born or at your young age which will affect how you will end the journey of your life. For example if you are building a house and the foundation has a problem, watch the building, it might take some years after years, but one day, the house will begin to collapse. If a child was born and dedicated to water spirit or demons, that means such child destiny has already be tampered with and for that child to exhibit a good attitude will be difficult.

Most first born who manifest faulty foundation are mostly under challenges, like going around the circle, financial hardship, untimely death, late marriages, wrong relationships, hate going to church, school dropout, set back, disappointments, poverty, sickness addiction to drugs, and mental challenges.

There are some parents that their lineage worship Idols and idol worshippers have a demonic spirit programmed to destroy destinies. Also, there are some ancestors that have also killed innocent lives and as a result of this effect, their firstborn could suffer the consequences of their evil acts.

This is the main reason, every first born needs to pray and always denounce, renounce and break free from the evil attachments from those evil spirits. Do you notice that first born are always making errors or mistakes?.

The only way the powers of the evil foundation can operate to destroy the destiny of the first born is to make such person to make error so the wicked powers can fulfill their purpose. The reason for such errors is that the gods of their ancestors will program wrong husbands, wives, wrong friends, jobs, businesses, schools and wrong environments, so that such person will not fulfill his or her destiny.

God instructed Abraham to leave his father's house to a land of settlement because Abraham's father was an Idol worshiper. Based upon the faulty foundation of Abraham, his wife Sarah was barren, Isaac's wife Rebekah was barren and Jacob's wife Rachel was also barren until God's divine intervention. As long, the child is able to identify the wrongs of his or her foundation and wrong behavior, and the child pray and turn from his or her evil ways, God is able to overturn, overturn and overturn evil judgment and make such child to begin to fulfill great destiny.

WARNING TO PARENTS: If your first born is doing wrong things, please, don't pronounce curse upon the child.

The spirit operating in the foundation of his or her life cannot work against their destiny expect the child misbehave and then the evil spirit will use parents or someone to pronounce a curse upon the child. Every parents should be knowledgeable that it is a spiritual battle when a child is misbehaving. Declare a positive declaration of God's word on the child.

Once a curse is unleashed, the destiny of such child is negatively affected. Pray for your first born regardless of whatever the child does and expect God to intervene.

BIBLICAL CASES OF THOSE WHO SINNED AND THE CONSEQUENCE THAT RESULTED IN DEATH

"For, lo, thou shalt conceive, and bear a son; and no razor shall come on his head: for the child shall be a Nazarite unto God from the womb: and he shall begin to deliver Israel out of the hand of the Philistines" (Judges 13:5).

Samson was an anointed child from birth. A nazarite to be to deliver the Israelites from the hand of the philistines. He was also a judge in Israel for twenty years. However Samson went to Gaza and slept with a harlot and that was when he lost his spiritual, physical strength and his divine calling.

"Then went Samson to Gaza, and saw there an harlot, and went in unto her" (Judges 16:1). This is the consequence of the sin that resulted to his death.

"And Samson said, Let me die with the Philistines. And he bowed himself with all his might; and the house fell upon the lords, and upon all the people that were therein. So the dead which he slew at his death were more than they which he slew in his life." (Judges 16:30).

Generational curses, and errors are like unlocked doors for Satan to come in and perform his evil work. It is imperative to understand that these negative influence create an opportunity to harm first born's destiny. We need to safeguard ourselves from this kind of danger by being vigilant and aware of the potential risks. This is why individual person's needs to be careful of how you treat people. Life is a seed. Whatever you do to people whether good or bad, will come back to you. It is law of Karma. Do not let Satan have a foothold in your life; stay strong and keep your guard up to protect yourself. If a curse remains unaddressed within a family, the forces of darkness can wreak havoc for future generations. This means bad things happen to innocent children, which is just not fair. It is crucial to break any curses that might be lurking in your bloodline so that you and your loved ones can live happy, and healthy lives without the fear of harm or tragedy. Do not let the forces of darkness win—take action today!

Generational curses can affect everyone in a family but skip one that determined to break such curses. For example in a lineage when someone pronounce a curse that no one will marry and out of five in a family, only one was able to break the barriers and get married.

Jabez in the bible originated from an idolatry background that no one prosper in their family expect Jabez, who determined to change his name in order to break his generational curse

"And Jabez was more honorable than his brethren: and his mother called his name Jabez, saying, because I bare him with sorrow. And Jabez called on the God of Israel, saying, Oh that thou wouldest bless me indeed, and enlarge my coast, and that thine hand might be with me, and that thou wouldest keep me from evil, that it may not grieve me! And God granted him that which he requested." 1 Chron.4: 9-10.

God does not take no pleasure in making the destiny of a man so terrible, but a person can suffer consequences when he or she decided to engage in a bad life style that would shut the heaven of such person.

- ## PAY ATTENTION TO ERRORS

The spirit of error can stop a person who has a great destiny to be ruined. It is very disheartening to see so many children getting involved in gangs at school. What is particularly worrisome is the potential for individuals to become ensnared in the realm of darkness as a result of this situation.

The phenomenon can be likened to a gateway that facilitates the influx of various negative influences, thereby exposing young individuals to a perilous trajectory. We need to undertake all possible measures to avert the occurrence of this event. We need to educate our children about the potential hazards associated with gang involvement, while simultaneously offering constructive alternatives through intervention.

Let us collaborate to ensure the safety of our communities and safeguard our youth from the perils of evil.

Reasons parents can transfer curses upon their children

And Ahab spake unto Naboth, saying, Give me thy vineyard, that I may have it for a garden of herbs, because it is near unto my house: and I will give thee for it a better vineyard than it; or, if it seem good to thee, I will give thee the worth of it in money.
And Naboth said to Ahab, The LORD forbid it me, that I should give the inheritance of my fathers unto thee.

4 And Ahab came into his house heavy and displeased because of the word which Naboth the Jezreelite had spoken to him: for he had said, I will not give thee the inheritance of my fathers. And he laid him down upon his bed, and turned away his face, and would eat no bread.

And he said unto her, Because I spake unto Naboth the Jezreelite, and said unto him, Give me thy vineyard for money; or else, if it please thee, I will give thee another vineyard for it: and he answered, I will not give thee my vineyard.

And Jezebel his wife said unto him, Dost thou now govern the kingdom of Israel? arise, and eat bread, and let thine heart be merry: I will give thee the vineyard of Naboth the Jezreelite.

So she wrote letters in Ahab's name, and sealed them with his seal, and sent the letters unto the elders and to the nobles that were in his city, dwelling with Naboth.

And she wrote in the letters, saying, Proclaim a fast, and set Naboth on high among the people:

And set two men, sons of Belial, before him, to bear witness against him, saying, Thou didst blaspheme God and the king. And then carry him out, and stone him, that he may die.

And the men of his city, even the elders and the nobles who were the inhabitants in his city, did as Jezebel had sent unto them, and as it was written in the letters which she had sent unto them.

They proclaimed a fast, and set Naboth on high among the people.

And there came in two men, children of Belial, and sat before him: and the men of Belial witnessed against him, even against Naboth, in the presence of the people, saying, Naboth did blaspheme God and the king. Then they carried him forth out of the city, and stoned him with stones, that he died.

Then they sent to Jezebel, saying, Naboth is stoned, and is dead.

And it came to pass, when Jezebel heard that Naboth was stoned, and was dead, that Jezebel said to Ahab, Arise, take possession of the vineyard of Naboth the Jezreelite, which he refused to give thee for money: for Naboth is not alive, but dead.

And it came to pass, when Ahab heard that Naboth was dead, that Ahab rose up to go down to the vineyard of Naboth the Jezreelite, to take possession of it.

And the word of the LORD *came to Elijah the Tishbite, saying, Arise, go down to meet Ahab king of Israel, which is in Samaria: behold, he is in the vineyard of Naboth, whither he is gone down to possess it.*

And thou shalt speak unto him, saying, Thus saith the LORD, *Hast thou killed, and also taken possession? And thou shalt speak unto him, saying, Thus saith the* LORD, *In the place where dogs licked the blood of Naboth shall dogs lick thy blood, even thin.And Ahab said to Elijah, Hast thou found me, O mine enemy? And he answered, I have found thee: because thou hast sold thyself to work evil in the sight of the* LORD. *Behold, I will bring evil upon thee, and will take away thy posterity, and will cut off from Ahab him that pisseth against the wall, and him that is shut up and left in Israel,*

And will make thine house like the house of Jeroboam the son of Nebat, and like the house of Baasha the son of Ahijah, for the provocation wherewith thou hast provoked me to anger, and made Israel to sin.

And of Jezebel also spake the LORD, saying, The dogs shall eat Jezebel by the wall of Jezreel. Him that dieth of Ahab in the city the dogs shall eat; and him that dieth in the field shall the fowls of the air eat. But there was none like unto Ahab, which did sell himself to work wickedness in the sight of the LORD, whom Jezebel his wife stirred up.

And he did very abominably in following idols, according to all things as did the Amorites, whom the LORD cast out before the children of Israel. And it came to pass, when Ahab heard those words, that he rent his clothes, and put sackcloth upon his flesh, and fasted, and lay in sackcloth, and went softly. And the word of the LORD came to Elijah the Tishbite, saying, Seest thou how Ahab humbleth himself before me? because he humbleth himself before me, I will not bring the evil in his days: but in his son's days will I bring the evil upon his house". 1 Kings 21:1-28

Based on this scriptures, many children are product or victims of curses due to the sins of their father or mother. Ahab was a wicked king who misuse his power to covert the vineyard of his neighbor Naboth.

Naboth informed king Ahab that the land was an inheritance of his father to him, but king Naboth refused to listen to him and the king reported to his wicked wife Jezebel about Naboth refusal to give him his inheritance. So, Jezebel king Ahab's wife was upset because Naboth refused to relinquish the land. So, king Ahab wife Jezebel wrote a letter to the elders and nobles and lied against Naboth. Unfortunately the elder did not ask about the offense Naboth committed and the elders and nobles carried a death instruction from Jezebel and Naboth was stoned to death. After the death of Naboth, Kind Ahab went to take the possession of Naboth.

I pray what belongs to you, your first born or children will not be forcefully taken.

(In verse 17), Elijah the Tishbite was instructed by God to king Ahab and and when Elijah explained to king Ahab that in the place where dogs licked the blood of Naboth shall dogs lick King Ahab's blood. Immediately, King Ahab rent his clothes, and put sack cloth upon his flesh, fasted and lay in sackcloth. King Ahab repented of the death crime to Naboth. An instruction was given to Elijah the Tishbite that, since Ahab humbled himself before God, the Lord said, he not bring the evil in his days but he will bring the evil to his son's days.

"See how Ahab has humbled himself before Me? Because he has humbled himself before Me, I will not bring the calamity in his days. In the days of his son I will bring the calamity on his house." 1 Kings 21:29. If you want your children to fulfill their destiny, then every parents must learn to treat people in a godly manner. Everyone will reap whatsoever you sow into people's life.

HOW ERRORS CAN DESTROY GREAT DESTINIES

- Reuben was the first born of Jacob and he committed an error and his father Jacob cursed him, saying, *"Unstable as water, you shall not excel, because you went up to your father's bed; Then you defiled it—He went up to my couch."* Genesis 49:4. NKJ
- David was furious with Joab for killing Abner and David cursed him for it. This is recorded in 2 Samuel 3:28–29.
- Similarly, Noah cursed his son Ham after he made a mistake, as described in Genesis 9:25–26.
- Tragically, Amnon was killed by his own brother Absalom after he had committed a terrible crime against their half-sister Tamar. The incident serves as a reminder of the dangers of unchecked desire and the destructive power of jealousy within families (2 Samuel 13:1–15).

It is imperative to bear in mind that our actions have consequences, and it is incumbent upon us to exercise prudence in our conduct. Through consistent prayer and seeking guidance from God, can avoid making mistakes and preventing our children from deviating from the right path.

As a parent, it is crucial to engage in prayer and seek protection against any generational curses that may have been transmitted through the family lineage. This way, you can prevent negative forces from getting in the way of your children's future success. Don't be afraid to intervene and protect your children's paths to greatness, especially your firstborn.

WHY FIRSTBORNS ARE UNDER ATTACK

In the book of Job 1:6–12, it is evident that there is nothing that happens in the earthly realm that has not been concluded or programmed in the spirit realm. Recently, there has been a trend of targeting and attacking firstborns.

Why?
From the beginning, since the days of Adam, the firstborn has been under constant spiritual attacks. This includes being separated from God's presence, blessings, and provisions.

It's crucial to comprehend the reasons behind these attacks and how we can safeguard ourselves from them. Adam was banished from God's presence due to **DISOBEDIENCE.**

Firstborns are subjected to spiritual attacks because of their flawed nature. This is exemplified by Cain's act of murdering his own brother, Abel. He was banished from God's presence and suffered the consequences of his actions. It is important to acknowledge our shortcomings and seek redemption through faith and repentance.

- In Exodus 11:5, God warned of a coming plague that would strike all the firstborns of Egypt. Perhaps, these attacks on firstborns are a reflection of the ongoing spiritual battle between good and evil. It's crucial that we remain steadfast in our faith and trust in God's protection during these trying times.
- The birth and death of Jesus Christ had already been concluded and planned before they were executed in the earthly realm. According to the Gospel of Matthew 2:1–12, wise men saw a star signifying the arrival of Jesus and went to visit him. When they told Herod about their journey, he became jealous and felt threatened by this new king.

- In an attempt to retain his authority, Herod commanded the slaughter of all male infants, including Jesus. This is why some believe that firstborns may encounter distinct spiritual challenges.

- Whenever we succumb to temptation and commit a sin, we lose God's grace. Eventually, we may feel ashamed of our actions. The Bible teaches that we were created to be perfect, but once sin enters the picture, it can corrupt even the most righteous. Ezekiel 28:15 clearly states this truth.

As a concerned parent, you should discourage your university- or college-aged children from joining social clubs such as fraternities and sororities. These organizations have the potential to steer your child astray from God's path toward sinful activities like partying, secret meetings, and sexual promiscuity. These clubs have unique symbols and identifiers that foster a feeling of exclusivity and separation from others. It is crucial to prioritize your child's spiritual well-being over any potential benefits or social status that may come from joining such groups.

I pray that you receive the amazing power of the Holy Spirit. May His Spirit protect you from any harmful plans designed to ruin your future.

As stated in Luke 1:35, let this divine guidance lead you towards success and keep you away from anything that can take you off God's path in Jesus name.

However, the very day the Lord opens their eyes to comprehend the purpose behind their afflictions, the problem or challenge will be over. God has a unique plan for our firstborn, but when there is a demonic opening, then the devil is empowered to operate. I pray that anyone reading this book will be set free by God will be able to fulfill his or her destiny in Jesus' name. Amen!

Testimony

There was a testimony of a young boy who was under a spiritual attack due to the fetish powers. When the young boy was born, the grandmother gave the boy the first bath, something strange happened to him. The boy couldn't breathe, so he was rushed to a native doctor. The herbalist used his demonic power to relive the boy back to life.

During the period, the boy was supposed to go to high school, he will skip school and sit by the side of river. The parents scolded him and then, he finished his high school. Immediately he entered college, he joined the occult group and the boy started to fight with knives and he also was sleeping with different ladies. The boy could not keep a job nor engaged in any business. The herbalist dedicated the boy to water spirit and spirit wife that triggered his misbehavior. Another evil spirit was given as a guidance to the boy.

Up till now the boy refused to go to church and so, parents gave up on him. When I got to know about the problem the boy was facing, I took his name to my alter for prayer and I had a dream of the boy sitting down on an edge of a bed and another old man was sitting in another edge of a bed watching him. I asked the boy why was he sitting down in the bed, he said the old man detained him and he cannot run. The boy also told me in the dream he does not like the bad habit he's exhibiting but he cannot help himself. I told his parents to take him to church and pray for him instead of releasing curses upon him. If your challenges is too difficult, then you need to ask questions from your parents and learn to live a righteous life.

Have you ever wondered why your first child experiences more spiritual battles than their siblings? This may be because someone saw a special star in him or her and decreed evil words into their life. Don't leave your child to fight these battles alone. Seek guidance and support to help them overcome these obstacles.

Testimony

There was a young lady very pretty and had a great destiny. Unfortunately, during her adolescent, she had an altercation with her mother and her mother brought out her breast and placed a curse upon her first born and her mother said "Her daughter will never have peace". Her daughter laughed when her mother pronounced the curse upon her daughter. During the time for the daughter to settle down for marriage, her marital destiny was exchanged. She married to a wrong man who will beat her and that eventually led to divorced. When this lady went to college, a bird flew inside the classroom which made the lady dizzied, and immediately she developed a headache. That was the end of college. She couldn't complete her school, so she ended as a dropout.. Her friends pitted her and put money together to start a business, but the business failed. At the moment she realized her mistake it was too late.

She apologized to her mother of her mistakes but the mother did not accept the apology. So, the lady continued been miserable. She couldn't access help from anyone rather bitterness. The lady tried to commit suicide until someone connected her to a pastor to pray for her. The pastor instructed her to buy gift and give her mother money to pray for her. The lady followed the instruction and the mother later prayed for her and things started working together for her good.

A lot of children do not have a clue the danger of abusing or fighting their parents or an elder. If any child wants to fulfill his or her purpose in their journey of life, be disciplined to show respect to higher authority.

Another Story

A very young lady in college dated a man who was an occultist without knowing who the man was. The man lavished money on the girl and the man proposed to her for marriage. The lady agreed to marry him. But unfortunately, this girl met another wealthy young guy that proposed to her and immediately, she married the guy. When the occultist man learnt about what the girl did, he told the girl that she will never have a settled husband. Eventually, the curse worked against the lady. Every new marriage to a man results to divorced.

These are lessons that all college student and young girls and boys must be careful of whom they date or who proposed to them. All our children needs to be born again and pray before getting into any relationship.

The bible says *"The steps of a good man are ordered by the LORD"* (Psalm 37:23). If your ways are right you will be like a tree planted by the rivers of water, that bringeth forth his fruit in his season; his leaf also shall not wither, and whatsoever he doeth shall prosper (Psalm 1:3).

For every man to fulfill destiny, you need to be connected to the Holy Spirit and it is the spirit of God that direct your path from errors.

WHY IS THE FIRSTBORN SO IMPORTANT IN THE FAMILY?

- Firstborns are the first offspring to come into this world.
- The firstborn is the holder of the star and is the first to emerge from the mother's womb.
- They set an example for younger siblings to follow and look up to.
- First-born children often bear the burden of being the trailblazers in navigating life's challenges, which includes learning from their parents' mistakes as well as their own.
- Firstborns can be both a blessing and a curse, as they may feel pressured to succeed and set standards for future generations.
- In certain cultures and religions, the firstborn holds a unique position in terms of family history, tradition, inheritance, and leadership roles.

- For the Firstborns, with great importance comes great responsibility, and the potential for generational curses or blessings to be passed down through them.

It's crucial to spend time praying and breaking negative generational cycles. By doing this, we can ensure a positive and blessed future for our children, free from the same struggles and obstacles faced by their forefathers.

Let us act today to break free from the shackles of our past and pave the way for a brighter tomorrow.

I declare in the powerful name of Jesus, with His mercy and by His blood, that any wicked force or darkness seeking to ruin or alter the destiny of your firstborn will be reversed and transformed into positive outcomes, in Jesus' name. Amen!

SIGNS YOUR FIRST BORN NEED DIVINE INTERVENTION

These are circumstances or challenges that indicate the necessity for earnest prayer or divine intervention from God concerning your firstborn.

1. When an individual experiences a pattern of unsuccessful marriages or a lack of accomplishments.

2. When your firstborn noticed that him or her does not have a relationship with God and hate reading the Bible or engaging in prayer.

3. When an individual consistently experiences failure, misfortune, illness, financial hardship, social rejection, lack of progress in personal relationships or career, involvement in criminal activity, substance abuse, or persistent anxiety.

4. When an individual frequently and consistently relies on borrowing funds from others, including siblings.

5. When you notice that no man has approached your adult firstborn daughter to ask for her hand in marriage.

6. When an individual observes a consistent lack of success in their endeavors, despite their efforts.

7. When your firstborn noticed that him or her helps others to succeed, but when it comes to themselves, they are always stagnant, and nothing good comes on their way.

8. When an individual consistently experiences feelings of agitation and displays a tendency to engage in confrontational behavior with those in their immediate environment, it may be indicative of an underlying issue.

9. When you observe your firstborn lacks good manners, and they are disrespectful.

10. The individual consistently experiences negative dream content and never have victory over negative dreams.

11. When they are constantly dreaming of people chasing them in the dreams and they are defeated.

12. When an individual invests in good things but achieves little.

13. If you notice your parents were idol worshippers or you are aware that you come from a polygamous home.

14. The presence of a faulty foundation has been observed.

15. When you as a parent noticed your firstborn join gangs and him or her have been initiated through blood covenant.

> **The listed nuggets will help you to stay on the right line for your spiritual journey.**

- You must surrender your life to Jesus Christ (1 John 5:4-6).
- Live a life of holiness (Romans 12:1-2).
- Study, meditate, and memorize the Word of God (Joshua 1:18).

- Confess your sins and repent from sinning against God (Proverbs 28:13).
- Let pastor dedicate you to God in a church with a anointing oil and sow a seed for your destiny (Exodus 13:1-16) (Exodus 34:20).
- Let pastor pray for you and destroy curses that follow first born in your family (Galatians 3:13).
- Learn Christian songs and learn to worship and praise God (Psalm 96:1–3).
- Look for a Holy Ghost-filled church and join a department (be visible in the church) (Psalm 92:13).
- Engage in constant night vigil prayer from midnight (Acts 16:25–26).
- Be responsible and be accountable in your actions.

Scriptures To Guide You During Prayer For Your First Born.

Isaiah 30:21: "Whether you turn to the right or to the left, your ears will hear a voice behind you, saying", "This is the way; walk in it".

Galatians 3:13: "Christ has redeemed us from the curse of the law, being made a curse for us, for it is written, Cursed is everyone that hangeth on the tree"

Ezekiel 36:26: "I will give you a new heart and put a new spirit in you; I will remove from you your heart of stone and give you a heart of flesh".

Obadiah 1:17: "But upon Mount Zion shall be deliverance, and there shall be holiness; and the house of Jacob shall possess their possessions".

Ezekiel 36:34–36: "The desolate land shall be tilled instead of lying desolate in the sight of all who pass by".

35) So they will say, "This land that was desolate has become like the garden of Eden; and the wasted, desolate, and ruined cities are now fortified and inhabited".

36) "Then the nations which are left all around you shall know that I, the Lord, have rebuilt the ruined places and planted what was desolate. I, the Lord, have spoken it, and I will do it".

Proverbs 4:14: "Enter not into the path of the wicked, and go not in the way of evil men".

Isaiah 8:18: "Behold, I and the children whom the LORD hath given me are for signs and for wonders in Israel from the LORD of hosts, which dwelleth in Mount Zion".

Isaiah 54:17: "No weapon that is formed against thee shall prosper, and every tongue that shall rise against thee in judgment thou shalt condemn. This is the heritage of the servants of the LORD, and their righteousness is of me, saith the LORD".

Numbers 23:23: "Surely there is no enchantment against Jacob, neither is there any divination against Israel: according to this time it shall be said of Jacob and of Israel, what hath God wrought!"

Psalm 64:1-2: "Oh that thou wouldest rend the heavens, that thou wouldest come down, that the mountains might flow down at thy presence, As when the melting fire burneth, the fire causeth the waters to boil, to make thy name known to thine adversaries, that the nations may tremble at thy presence!"

Isaiah 60:1-2: "Arise, shine; for thy light is come, and the glory of the Lord is risen upon thee, For, behold, the darkness shall cover the earth, and gross darkness the people: but the Lord shall arise upon thee, and his glory shall be seen upon thee".

Proverbs 4:18: "But the path of the just is as the shining light, that shineth more and more unto the perfect day".

Galatians 6:17: *"From henceforth let no man trouble me: for I bear in my body the marks of the Lord Jesus"*.

Romans 8:37: *"Nay, in all these things we are more than conquerors through him that loved us"*.

Jeremiah 29:11: *"For I know the plans I have for you,' declares the Lord, 'plans to prosper you and not to harm you, plans to give you a hope and a future"*.

Isaiah 54:13-16: *"All your children shall be taught by the Lord, and great shall be and the peace of your children. In righteousness, you shall be established; you shall be far from oppression, for you shall not fear; and from terror, for it shall not come near you. Indeed, they shall surely assemble, but not because of Me. Whoever assembles against you shall fall for your sake. Behold, I have created the blacksmith who blows the coals in the fire, who brings forth an instrument for his work, and I have created the spoiler to destroy."*

Isaiah 8:18: "Behold, I and the children whom the LORD hath given me are for signs and for wonders in Israel from the LORD of hosts, which dwelleth in mount Zion".

Psalm 112:2-3: "His descendants will be mighty on earth; the generation of the upright will be blessed. Wealth and riches will be in his house, and his righteousness endures forever. Unto the upright there ariseth light in the darkness: he is gracious, and full of compassion, and righteous".

Psalm 141:9-10: "Keep me from the snares which they have laid for me, and the gins of the workers of iniquity. Let the wicked fall into their own nets, whilst that I withal escape.
If my people which are called by my name, shall humble themselves and pray and seek my face, and turn from their wicked ways; then will I hear from heaven and will forgive their sin, and will heal their land

Psalm 23:1-6 KJV: "The LORD *is my shepherd; I shall not want. He maketh me to lie down in green pastures: he leadeth me beside the still waters. He restored my soul: he leaded me in the paths of righteousness for his name's sake. Yea, though I walk through the valley of the shadow of death, I will fear no evil: for thou art with me; thy rod and thy staff they comfort me. Thou prepares a table before me in the presence of mine enemies: thou anointment my head with oil; my cup runneth over. Surely goodness and Mercy shall follow me all the days of my life: and I will dwell in the house of the* LORD *forever.*

Prayer Points For First Born

➤ Father, in the name of Jesus Christ, I thank you for the battles you won for me, thank you for the salvation of my soul, gifts of life, health, job, business and grace to always approach your throne of mercy.

➤ *"If my people, which are called by my name shall humble themselves and pray and seek my face and turn from their wicked ways, then will I hear from heaven, and will forgive their sin, and will heal their land"* (2 chron. 7-14). Father, have mercy upon me as a first born, I repent from all my sin that empowers evil altars against me, wash me from the filthiness of the mind. Create in me a new heart and a new spirit, so that I can follow your instructions and fulfill destiny.

➤

Thou shalt not bow down thyself unto them, nor serve them; for I, the LORD thy God, am a jealous God, visiting the iniquity of the fathers upon the children unto the third and fourth generation of them that hate Me (Deuteronomy 5:9). O Lord, you are good and ready to forgive and plenteous in mercy unto all them that call upon you. Turn unto me and have mercy for the sins committed by my fathers, mothers, both sides of my family and up to the fourth generations and let there be a lifting for me.

➤ *And the blood shall be to you for a token upon the houses where ye are: and when I see the blood, I will pass over you, and the plague shall not be upon you to destroy you, when I smite the land of Egypt.* (Exodus 12:13). I turn myself into the Holy Ghost fire. I bear in my body the mark of the blood of Jesus Christ, no evil or plague shall come near me. My times and seasons are protected from evil monitoring spirit.

➤ Dear Lord, as the one who shapes our paths and mends our brokenness, I pray that you heal my children's wounds with your loving touch *(Jeremiah 17:14).* Free them from any shackles that hold them back, just like you rescued us from danger in Psalm 124:7. Please revive anything in their lives that may have felt lifeless or hopeless (Jeremiah 30:8), so they can live out the destiny you have intended for them. Amen.

- Every waster of destiny monitoring my firstborn for an untimely death, hear the word of the Lord: My redeemer is strong, and the Lord of hosts is His name; I waste you today; I frustrate you today in the name of Jesus (Isaiah 49:2).

- I separate my firstborn from everything they have inherited: bad habits, sicknesses, evil patterns, and curses, in the mighty name of Jesus (Psalms 142:7).

- Oh Lord, by your mercy, deliver my firstborn from unfriendly friends, deliver him or her from wrong counsels, and grant them your discerning spirit at all times in Jesus' mighty name (Psalm 41:9–10; Psalm 144:11)

- May the Lord guide me and every step transition I make, lead me towards righteousness.

- May I trust in your divine plan and follow the path with faith and courage.

- May God's love and grace be upon me always, guiding me through life's journey with peace and joy.

- I confess that lines will fall to me in pleasant places.

- The excellent spirit of God manifest in my life so therefore, as the firstborn I will do excellently well in all grades.

- As the first born, I receive wisdom, and will walk in the dominion and favor of the Lord. (Isaiah 61:9).

- I dedicate my minds, imaginations, and emotions to God the Father, Son, and Holy Ghost in Jesus mighty name.

- As the firstborn I refuse evil and choose good.

- (Isaiah 7:15–16) Oh, my glory, awakes early.

- (Psalms 57:8; Psalms 90:14): I decree that all the good things that never worked for me begin to work. All the good things that stopped working, come back to life in Jesus mighty name.

- THERE SHALL BE NO DELAY OR SLOW PROGRESS FOR MY FIRSTBORN (mention his or her name).

- In righteousness, I will be established and be far away from oppression (Isaiah 54:14).

- As the first born, I shall be mighty on the earth, and my generation shall be blessed.

- No weapon formed against my first born shall prosper (Psalm 112:2).

- May the Lord break every band of wickedness, undo heavy burdens, addiction, generational curses, errors, sin, and any hidden yoke from my life and set me free.

- My destiny shall break forth (Isaiah 58:6–8).

- May the Lord enlarge the place of my dwelling and may I stretch forth my habitation, in Jesus' name. (Isaiah 54:2).

- I command my blood, pictures, name, property, fingernails, hair and my image become Holy Ghost fire in any coven.

- Any time my name is mentioned for evil, let the Holy Ghost fire answer on my behalf.

- The spirit of the Most High shall overshadow me and teach me the way of the Lord (Luke 1:45).

- May the Lord give me a new heart and put His new spirit in me. May the Lord remove the heart of stone and give me a heart of flesh so that I can pant after God all the days of my life.

- I thank God for being the hiding place for my life, for preserving him or her from trouble, and for instructing, and teaching them the way to go (Psalm 32:7-8).

- I declare into my of my life as the firstborn, the Lord shall be my defense; the Lord will anoint me for greatness; wisdom and understanding will my portions, and the enemy will not exact to afflict me. (Psalm 89:22).

- The Lord will exalt, promote, and bring me to honor. I declare that I will not enter the path of the wicked or encounter bad friends, but my part will be of the just man, like a shining light that shines and shines more and more to the perfect day (Proverbs 4:14–18).

> The Lord will satisfy me early with his mercy. I will marry at the appropriate time, without delay. I will finish my academic work at the right time; there will be no carryover and I shall marry a godly spouse to have a good home, in Jesus' name (Psalm 90:14).

> I speak to my destiny as the firstborn that I will number my days and apply my hearts to wisdom (Psalm 90:12).

> As the firstborn, I shall not be a father or mother who labors and dies at the beginning of my labor

> **"And I, the Lord, will be their God, and my servant David a prince among them; I, the Lord, have spoken it". (Ezekiel 34:24).** I decree that the Lord will be your God—martially, academically, spiritually, mentally—and perfect everything that concerns you in the name of Jesus Christ.

➢ *"Moreover, I will appoint a place for My people Israel, and I will plant them, that they may dwell in a place of their own and move no more, where the son of the wicked will not locate you".* (2 Samuel 7:10). Father, in the name of Jesus Christ, appoint a place for me as the firstborn, appoint the right friends, appoint the right house to buy, appoint the right career, appoint the right school, appoint the right job, appoint the right business, and appoint the right church to serve you all the days of the my life, and no power of darkness shall locate me

➢ O Lord, arise and have mercy upon me for the time to favor me the set time has come (Psalm 102-13).

➢ *"Now thanks be unto God, which always causeth us to triumph in Christ"* (2 Cor.2:14). I decree as the firstborn by the grace of God, I shall triumph over addiction, and evil desire of the flesh and I declare victory is won in the journey of my life in Jesus name.

➢ By the blood of the everlasting covenant, I break free from every generational curse from my father's and mother's house. I disconnect from the idols of my father's house. I decree that any enchantment or divination programmed against my life and destiny shall catch fire and return back to the sender in Jesus' name.

➢ As the firstborn, I will serve the Lord all the days of my life. I disconnect myself from the ordinance of idol, sorority, fraternity group and evil association. I decree Jesus Christ shall be my savior thought the journey of my life. (Joshua 24:15)

➢ *We overcome them by the blood of the lamp and by the word of our testimony.* (Rev. 12:11) By the blood of the everlasting covenant, let the blood Jesus Christ visit every operations of poverty, shame, setback, merry go round and every spirit assigned to stop your destiny. I come on the backing of God's grace to destroy such evil assignment, I decree death to any enactment and divination working against you, I shut the power of the moon, sun, wind and earth against them.

- My destiny, glory, my times and seasons, I connect you to the throne of grace, altars of God's glory, honor, favor, goodness, joy and the blessing of God. I decree from today, I am not connected to the limitation of the blood line. I decree from now, I switch from darkness to loyalty of Christ Jesus.

- Any system of authorization as a result of personal sin, territorial sin, foundation sin from the blood line, I called the mercy of God that every legal hold over my firstborn is hereby broken (x7).

- By the power in the name of Jesus Christ, any evil wicked powers that is waiting for the day of my honor, Holy Ghost destroy you. Nothing can stop my lifting.

- I dethrone every princes of this world assigned to war against my destiny. Your hands shall not be able to fulfill your plans. My destiny, hear the word of God, arise and shine.

- Fire from Heaven burn to ashes every evil calender drafted to change my star. I speak to the calender of my destiny, the kindness of God shall not depart from me (Isaiah 54:10).

➤ I decree every negative patterns, frequent evil occurrence that tried to stop me of my next level, patterns of delay, inferiority complex, I command an end to such evil activities of the wicked. I command you to a rise and shine to the world. I command your destiny to open to good things in Jesus name.

➤ I decree and declare that as the first born, I shall make heaven, The Lord will beautify my life with his favor. By God's grace, I am exempted from what affects other people. By God's grace, I shall escape the evil plans of men. By God's help, I will get what I am not qualified for. After praying all these prayers points, positive things will be attracted to me and I shall be victorious all the days of my life. Amen.

Chapter

2 DAILY INTERCESSION FOR CHILDREN

Daily Intercession
for Children

Isaiah 28:18, "And your covenant with death shall be disannulled, and your agreement with hell shall not stand".

Isaiah 43:18-19, "Remember ye not the former things, neither consider the things of old. Behold, I will do a new thing; now it shall spring forth; shall ye not know it? I will even make a way in the wilderness, and rivers in the desert".

Isaiah 54:14, "In righteousness shalt thou be established: thou shalt be far from oppression; for thou shalt not fear: and from terror; for it shall not come near thee".

Psalm: 112:2-4, "His seed shall be mighty upon earth: the generation of the upright shall be blessed".

Wealth and riches shall be in his house: and his righteousness endureth forever. Unto the upright there ariseth light in the darkness: he is gracious, and full of compassion, and righteous".

Psalm 91:10-11, "There shall no evil befall thee, neither shall any plague come nigh thy dwelling. For he shall give his angels charge over thee, to keep thee in all thy ways".

Based on these words of God:

➢ I denounce and renounce every evil covenant that my children must have entered into through sin and social media that have allowed an evil spirit to have access to their lives.

➢ I break every evil agreement made against my children's progress, and I decree they are free from every evil covenant. They will live to fulfill their destiny in Jesus' name.

➢ My children shall retain God's word and keep God's commandments, and they will live to fulfill their destiny.

➢ My children shall be taught by the Lord, and they shall be far away from every oppression.

- "No weapon formed against my children shall prosper."

- My children are mighty upon this earth, and their generation shall be blessed. Wealth and riches shall be in his house, and his righteousness endureth forever.

- I call my children out of spiritual prison of drug addiction and gangs. My children will not be found in prison but in an exhorted place of honor.

- "In righteousness shall my children be blessed"

- I disconnect my children from the evil foundation of their father's and mother's house.

- My children belong to the generation of the most blessed, and they shall live like kings on the earth.

- Every curse or spell from my parents transferred to me break right now in Jesus Name. x7

- My children will be mighty on the earth.

- My children will not enter the path of the wicked and will not go in the way of evil men.

➢ My children shall marry their right spouse, and they will be living like queens and kings on the earth.

➢ The rod of the wicked shall not rest upon my children. Whatever damage transferred from the blood line to your destiny, be repaired now by the blood of Jesus Christ.

➢ The Holy Ghost will protect and overshadow my children's dreams and let the seven spirit of God rest upon my children, wisdom, understanding, counsel, might, knowledge and fear of the Lord.

➢ I stand as a watchman for my children and I prophecy wealth, righteousness, fear of God, divine fulfillment and grace to end well. I shut the door against the forces that cut short the life of children early. I shut the door. (x7)

Thank you for answering prayer, in Jesus' name. Amen!

Chapter

3 COMMANDING YOUR DAY

3

Commanding Your Day

*"And have you ever ordered morning, 'Get up!'"
told Dawn, "Get to work!" So, you could seize
Earth like a blanket and shake out the wicked
like cockroaches? As the sun brings everything
to light, brings out all the colors and shapes, the
cover of darkness is snatched from the
wicked—they're caught in the very act!
(Job 38:12-15).*

The verses from Job 38:12–15 paint a powerful picture of how we should live each day and resist all forms of evil. It is important to take control of our day, even when bad things happen while we sleep. Sometimes, evil people will make sacrifices or submit names to an evil priest or shrine on behalf of others. We must stand firm against these dark forces and choose to do good instead. Let us seize the day and overcome any darkness that tries to bring us down.

The Bible says,

"But while men slept, his enemy came and sowed tares among the wheat and went his way." (Matthew 13:25)

The Bible warns us that if we are not diligent in prayer, the enemy can sneak in and plant harmful seeds. Before we know it, our lives may become stagnant or even endangered. It's crucial to take control of our day by declaring victory over the enemy's plans.

Prayer is a powerful weapon that we have been given to combat the schemes of the devil. It's not just a religious duty or tradition; it's a way of life for those who want to fulfill their destiny and purpose on this earth.

And one told David, saying, Ahithophel is among the conspirators with Absalom. And David said, O LORD, I pray thee, turn the counsel of Ahithophel into foolishness." (2 Sam.15:31)

King David would have been extinguished from this world, if he did not pray to overturn the counsel of Ahitophel.

Another example is the story of Harman who plotted to end the lives of the Jewish including queen Esther and Mordecai but because of prayer and fasting, God overturn the evil plan of Harman and he and his house hold died the death he planned for Mordecai and the Jewish

"So they hanged Haman on the gallows that he had prepared for Mordecai". (Esther 7:10)

When we pray, we connect with God and invite His presence and power into our lives. We declare our faith in Him and trust in His ability to guide us through any situation. We also acknowledge our dependence on Him and surrender our wills to His perfect plan for us. This attitude of humility and obedience attracts blessings and protection from above, as well as the discernment and wisdom to navigate the challenges of life.

Furthermore, prayer is not limited to a specific time or place, but is a continuous conversation with God throughout our day. We can pray while we work, drive, exercise, or even as we go about our daily routines. By inviting God into every moment of our lives, we become more aware of His presence and guidance. This allows us to live with a sense of purpose and direction, knowing that we are not alone in our struggles.

In conclusion, commanding your day is all about beginning each day with prayer and surrendering to God's will. Instead of letting circumstances dictate how we feel or react, we approach each situation with a sense of peace and confidence, knowing that God is in control. This not only brings us closer to Him, but also allows us to fulfill our purpose on earth by living a life that reflects His love and goodness.

Testimony

A sister went to work, and while driving, she felt a strong desire to connect with God. She called into the prayer line and poured her heart out in supplication. When she arrived home, something compelled her to stay in the car until she finished her prayer. To her shock, at the stroke of midnight, a rabbit emerged on the grassy lawn outside her house. The bunny stood motionless, facing directly towards her front door. Without hesitation, she stepped out of the vehicle and began to pray fervently. As if by divine intervention, the rabbit vanished into thin air as soon as she started praying.

This experience left this sister in awe and wonder at the power of prayer. It was a reminder to her that God is always listening and answering our prayers in ways we may not expect or understand. The appearance of the rabbit at midnight could have been seen as just a coincidence, but to her, it was a sign that God was present and watching over her.

This event strengthened her faith and gave her peace, knowing that no matter what happens in life, she can always turn to God for guidance and comfort.

Praise the Lord for this amazing sister who knows how to stand strong against evil forces. It turns out that the rabbit was a spy, working for those wicked people who know just when to strike. Why did the rabbit appear in the late hours of the night? Well, the evildoers understand that midnight is when most folks are sleeping soundly and unaware of the horrors lurking in the shadows. My prayer for you is that any plan hatched by the kingdom of darkness against you will be thwarted and defeated in Jesus' name.

Testimony

A few years back, I had a dream that shook me to my core. In the dream, I saw a man in the forest holding a lamp and walking around, and he had an oracle in his hand. He called out a name—a sister's name—that rang a bell with me as soon as I woke up at 1:30 am. God gave me this dream for a reason, and I realized that something sinister was happening to this woman. I started praying right away, trusting in God's word that says we can overcome anything with faith.

I shudder to think what would have happened if I hadn't prayed for her. The Bible reminds us that those who believe in God will triumph over the world. And let me tell you, every promise God makes to us will come true! So, keep your faith strong and trust that even in dark times, God has our backs.

Prayer Points to Command your Day

You are a child of the Most High, and all that is decreed will come to pass and God will give you a powerful testimony. By using these prayer points and scriptures to guide your day, you and your family members can conquer any evil plans meant to destroy your future. Trust in your faith and know that with God's help, nothing is impossible.

Song: There is power, there is power, there is power in the blood of Jesus.

Scriptures: *Psalm 5:1:3; Psalm 3:1-4; Psalm 2:1-5; Job 5:12; Number 23:23; 1 John 5:4.*

➤ Father, in the name of Jesus Christ, I exhort you and bless your name at all times. Thank you for waking me up, for saving my life from destruction during the night, and for granting me your loving kindness and tender mercies.

I give you all the glory, honor, and praise that you deserve. Amen. (Psalm 103:1-3).

➤ Dear Heavenly Father, thank you for this new day and for fighting my battles through the night. I pray in Jesus' name that you protect me from any harm or evil that may come my way today. I ask for your divine protection over my body, home, job, business, ministry, and career. May the blood of Jesus cover me with its protective shield wherever I go today. Thank you for your love and mercy. Amen.

➤ The Bible says, "Surely there is no enchantment against Jacob, nor is there any divination against Israel." (Numbers 23:23) By faith in Christ Jesus, I declare today that any curses or evil spells cast against me during the night will be destroyed by the Holy Ghost's fire. Amen!

➤ I decree in the authority of Jesus Christ, as I stand this morning for myself and for my family members, and I command every altar of delay, failure, stagnation, death, disfavor, rejection, get and loose, and any evil words spoken against my life and that of my family shall not stand.

➢ I declare that any harmful arrows aimed at me today will be sent back to the sender with multiplied force in the name of Jesus. Any wickedness lurking in rivers, graves, intersections, or other places around the world intended to harm me will be immediately uprooted and consumed by fire in Jesus' name.

➢ I am in control of the day and I command it to listen to me. With God's guidance, I declare that no element of the day will disrupt my plans or timing. Instead, they will align with His plan for my life. According to Jeremiah 29:11, God has a great purpose for me, and I trust Him to guide me through it all.

➢ Today, I declare that my family and I will experience God's peace, joy, favor, promotion, grace, protection, and blessings. I believe that these wonderful gifts from above will work in our lives today and beyond. In Jesus' name, amen!

➢ As it is written in the book of Jeremiah 52:32, the king showed great kindness to one man and gave him a seat above all others. In the name of Jesus Christ, I declare that God will guide me towards those who are meant to bring me success and fulfillment.

May their paths cross with mine, and may we work together towards greatness.

> I've chosen to follow Jesus Christ and make Him my Lord and Savior. Because of this, no destruction or challenge will come near my dwelling place. I command today that my household will not be swallowed up by life's challenges because I have decided to serve the almighty God regardless of the circumstances. I'll never get to a point in my life where I don't know how to get out.

> Today, I declare that the Lord will bring forth everything He has planned for me and my loved ones. With faith, I speak good things into existence for myself, my children, my spouse, my parents, and my siblings. The path ahead of us is blessed and full of promise.

> *Day unto day uttereth speech, and night unto night sheweth knowledge and there is no speech not language, where their voice is not heard* (Psalm 19:2-3). God speaks good things everyday concerning us, O good things of life that will channel me to my fulfillment locate and manifest in my life.

➤ I speak to the hour, second and minute of the day, , good news, email of good news, phone call of good news, good recommendation, my life is available, locate me and manifest.

Chapter

4

MID NIGHT PRAYERS

Mid Night Prayers

There is something sacred about praying in the middle of the night. Midnight prayer has been a practice for centuries and for good reason. No matter what your beliefs may be, there is no reason to deny the power of this timeless tool. So, the next time you find yourself awake in the wee hours, take a moment to offer up your own midnight prayer. You never know where it might lead.

There are a lot of evil occurrences going on that are imperceptible to the naked eye. As human beings, our perception of the world around us is limited. We rely heavily on our physical senses to navigate through life and make sense of our surroundings. However, there is a whole other dimension that exists beyond what we can perceive through our five senses. This realm is known as the *"spiritual realm"*.

It is during the midnight hour that negative transactions take place in this spiritual realm. The Bible refers to it as the *"watches of the night"* (Psalm 63:6). These are the hours between dusk and dawn when the forces of darkness are most active. It is during this time that we need to be vigilant and guard against any attacks from the enemy.

Midnight prayers offer us an opportunity to connect with God and seek His protection and guidance. It is a time for us to acknowledge our dependence on Him and surrender our fears and worries to Him. By praying at this critical hour, we can set ourselves up for victory over any evil occurrences that may come our way.

In conclusion, midnight prayers play a vital role in our spiritual journey. They allow us to tap into the power of prayer and commune with God during this crucial time when the forces of darkness are most active. Let us not underestimate the importance of these prayers and commit to making them a regular part of our daily routine.

A brother from Nigeria called for prayer in the middle of the night, scared and shaking because he had seen a group of evil birds flying around a tree near his house. They were making so much noise that it gave him goosebumps.

He quickly began to pray and recite scripture, calling on the power of Jesus Christ to protect him. The birds eventually flew away, but then an owl appeared, which is known to be even more powerful than those birds. The brother felt afraid once again and called me for help with prayer. We prayed together, asking for God's protection and strength against any evil forces trying to harm him.

The Scriptures already explain everything.

"But while men slept, his enemy came and sowed tares among the wheat and went his way". (Matthew 13:25)

Through unguided sleep, evil people sow evil seeds, such as sickness, death, limitations, shame, poverty, lack, divorce, miscarriage, rejection, and other problems, to their victims, especially when the wicked powers know your weaknesses.

"About midnight, Paul and Silas were praying and singing hymns to God, and the other prisoners were listening to them. Suddenly, there was such a violent earthquake that the foundations of the prison were shaken. At once all the prison doors flew open, and everyone's chains came loose." (Acts 16:25-26).

Paul and Silas found themselves in a dire situation. They were trapped in prison with chains binding their legs and hands, rendering them immobile. But they didn't lose hope. Even though they were unable to move, they knew they still had the power of prayer. With all their might, they prayed to God. And then something amazing happened: the power of God shook the very foundation of the prison and freed them from their captivity. It was a true testament to the strength of faith and perseverance, even in the toughest of times.

You might be facing an affliction, but do not let these situations or challenges prevent you from fellowshipping with God. The reason for this predicament is to distract you from advancing to the next level. When you engage in midnight prayer, there are angels who excel in strength and heed God's voice. Immediately, the warrior angels go to the very foundation of such a problem and begin to destroy it.

The reason God uses midnight to operate is that when you serve God in your own comfort time, nothing really works. But when you are engaged in doing things for God at a time when it is not convenient, that is when God shows up to do more than you can fathom. (Exodus 11:4).

Prayer Points for Mid Night Prayers

Song: I will sing unto the LORD, for he has triumphed gloriously, the horse and rider thrown into the sea.

Scriptures: *Psalm 91:1-16; Psalm 35 1-5; Psalm 21; Isaiah 8:9-10; Isaiah 7-1-7; Isaiah 54:17.*

1. Heavenly Father, I am grateful for your goodness and never-ending mercy. You showed your power by defeating the Egyptians and their firstborns, but even in that victory, your mercy remained steadfast. With joy in my heart, I sing praises to you because, through you, I have overcome the darkness of midnight. Hallelujah!

2. In the name of Jesus Christ, I command that our family shall dwell in the secret place of the Most High, and we shall abide under the shadow of the Almighty.

I will say of the Lord, You will be our refuge and our fortress. You will be our God, and in You, we will trust. Surely, God shall deliver us from the snare of the fowler and from the noisome pestilence. God shall cover us with his feathers, and under his wings shalt thou trust; his truth shall be our shield and buckler. (Psalm 91:1-6).

3. I release the brimstone of fire from heaven upon any witchcraft power visiting me at night in order to inflict any evil against me and my family, your time is over die by fire. (The bible says in Ex. 22:18 *"Suffer not a witch to live"*).

4. I command in the powerful name of Jesus Christ that all darkness and evil aimed towards me, my family, my belongings, and my present and future endeavors be bound right now. You will not be able to carry out your plans of harm or destruction against us. We declare God's protection over our lives day and night, shielded from any arrows of negativity. As it is written in Job 5:12, **"He thwarts the plans of the crafty so that their hands achieve no success."**

5. In the book of Ezekiel, it says that the king of Babylon is using divination to plan an attack on Jerusalem. He's shaking arrows, consulting images, and looking at the liver to make decisions. He plans to use battering rams and call for a slaughter against the city. However, those who have sworn oaths with him will see his divination as false. But God will bring their iniquity to light so they can be taken. I pray in Jesus' name that any satanic sacrifice prepared against me during the night is null and void through the word of God and the power of the Holy Ghost.

6. Holy ghost fire destroy every power of darkness assigned against me from the coven of water spirit, witches, wizard , spiritual wives, spiritual children, spiritual mirror, spiritual camera, spiritual satellites that the power of darkness are using to monitor me. Holy ghost fire destroy them x21.

7. Psalm 140:1, *"O Lord, keep me from the hands of the wicked; preserve me from the violent man, who have purposed to overthrow my goings"*. Every evil against me and my loved ones during the darkest hours of the night catch fire x7

8. Isaiah 28:18 says, ***"Your covenant with death will be annulled, and your agreement with Sheol will not stand; when the overflowing scourge passes through, then you will be trampled down by it."*** By the word of God, I return to the sender and destroy anyone who enters into any covenant with death over my life and the lives of my family. I shall not die but live to declare the glory of God.

9. Ezekiel 21:27 says, ***"Overthrown, overthrown, I will make it overthrown! It shall be no longer, until He comes, whose right it is, and I will give it to Him."*** May the Lord God overturn every evil plan against my life during the night, and I decree an outstanding testimony and favor to be following me all the days of my life.

10. Father, in the name of Jesus Christ, no more force of darkness shall be able to overcome me in the journey of my life. By the blood of Jesus Christ, I decree the four corners of the world will not cooperate with my enemy over my life in Jesus' name.

11. Thank you, Father, for not granting the desires of the wicked and not furthering his wicked device, lest they exalt themselves. (Psalm 140:8)

Thank you for answering my prayer. Amen!

Chapter

5 WHY MARRIAGE IS IMPORTANT

Why Marriage is Important

Marriage is a mutual relationship between two individuals who come together to become one flesh, and as you have entered into a covenant with God, they vow to remain together until death do them part. Many people no longer fulfill their vows, and each person will be held accountable to God on the day of judgment.

When God created Adam, He made Eve to be his helpmate, with the condition that both of them would become one flesh and not separate individuals (Genesis 2:18).

As a husband and wife, your relationship should be based on love, trust, support, and fear of God. Both partners should support each other in prayer. For a marriage to be successful, both partners need to study and meditate on God's word daily.

The presence of God in your lives will drive away every seen and unseen evil from your home. When prayer is unleashed, the Holy Spirit takes charge; therefore, the presence of God can reduce misunderstandings, prevent early divorce, and decrease verbal aggression.

There is an adage that says, "A family that prays together, stays together." This adage is true. When couples pray together, the Holy Spirit's presence instills a reverence for God in both individuals' hearts, preventing them from betraying or transgressing against each other.

The Bible says:

"The word of God have I hidden in mine heart, that I might not sin against thee". (Psalm 119:11-16 KJV)

The word of God is the spirit of God.

Prayer Points for Marriages

Song: What the Lord has done for me, I cannot tell it all.

Scriptures: *Matthew 19:6; Isaiah 54:17; Colossians 2:14; Rev. 12:11; Ezekiel 34:24—27; Deut. 11:12; Numbers 23:23.*

➢ I appreciate you, Lord, for your kindnesses that have never failed me. I sing unto the Lord a new song; for you have done marvelous things: his right hand and his holy arm have gotten me the victory. Over the kingdom of darkness.

➢ I pray for forgiveness of sin or any covenant that my parents or my ancestors have entered on my behalf or that I have entered that has affected my marriage. Lord Jesus, have mercy on us, and let the blood of the everlasting covenant cleanse me and make me whole.

> The bible says, "I overcame them by the blood of the lamp and the words of my testimony." Therefore, according to the Word of God, I overcome, denounce, and break every evil covenant or generational curse made on my behalf in regards to my marriage in Jesus' name. (Rev 12:11).

> In the name of Jesus Christ, I decree the blood of Jesus Christ to erase my marriage from the evil register of divorce, impossibility, limitation, miscarriage, untimely death, failure at the edge of breakthrough, shame, and stagnation. I now register my name in the book of honor, favor, fruitfulness, righteousness, wealth, peace, wisdom, mercy, marital breakthrough, success, stability, advancement, a long life, and good health. (Col.2:14).

> O Lord, make me go in the path of your commandments; incline my heart to your testimony and not to covetousness. Help me to turn my eyes from beholding vanity and quicken me in your way. Create in me a new heart, and let my spirit yearn for you at all times. (Psalm 51:10).

> O Lord, my father, I commit my marriage into your hands; preserve anything in our marriage appointed to die. I pray for unity and understanding to love and help each other as Christ has loved the church. (Psalm 79:11).

➤ Father, in the name of Jesus Christ, in our marriage, we shall build houses and inhabit them; we shall plant vineyards and eat our fruit. We shall not build and another inhabit; we shall not plant and another eat. I decree long life, and we shall enjoy the work of our hands in Jesus' name. (Isaiah 65:22).

➤ Father, in the name of Jesus Christ, I thank you for making a covenant of peace and understanding in my marriage and for getting rid of any external or internal affairs of the wicked against my home. (Ezekiel 34:25).

➤ Father, in the name of Jesus Christ, we receive power, grace, and anointing in our marriage against spiritual aborters, destiny exchangers, diversion, or perversion, and destiny hijackers. Our marriage shall not be aborted by the wicked ones in Jesus' name. (1 Corinthians 10:13).

Chapter

6 PRAYERS FOR SINGLES

6

Prayers for Singles

It is God's plan for you to marry at the right time and fulfill your destiny.

"For I know the plans I have for you, declares the LORD, "plans to prosper you and not to harm you, plans to give you hope and a future". Jeremiah 29:11

You have already been blessed from the day you were born because of the plans of God for you. God did not create you to be lonely and never marry. Unfortunately, there are many people who are not married or have not been attracted to their spouse. The reason is that the enemy, Satan, as well as evil people, can tamper with the plans of God towards you due to an early curse, generational curses, or a self-inflicted curse. If you notice that divorce runs in your family, it may be helpful to pray every day because spirits do not die. The spirit moves from generation to generation until someone prays to stop it.

There is this sister who told me that none of her siblings have ever been married. I instructed her to inquire about what happened to her during the time of her birth. The lady giving this testimony said that every time she asks her mother a marital question, her mother will change the subject. That means the mother knows why all of her children are not married. After a night vigil prayer, she had a strange dream about cobwebs all around her apartment. She also saw herself running in a huge river full of different reptiles, but God took her out like a wind and put her on dry land. After some months, a man called to propose to her. Never give up on prayer and living a holy life.

If you are having difficulty finding a spouse, do some inquiries from your parents and make sure to treat others with respect. Some ladies exhibit negative and unpleasant behavior, which may be a reason why some men don't want to marry them. Some ladies also engage in fornication and dress like prostitutes.

The Bible says,

"Search from the book of the Lord, and read: Not one of these shall fail; Not one shall lack her mate. For My mouth has commanded it, and His Spirit has gathered them." Isaiah 34:16.

Prayer Point for Singles

➢ *"Blessed be the Lord, who hath not given us as prey to their teeth. My soul has escaped as a bird out of the snare of the fowlers; the snare is broken, and I have escaped because my help is in the name of the Lord, who made heaven and earth".* (Psalm 124:6–8) Lord, I give you thanks for all you have done for me.

➢ O turn unto me, and have mercy upon me; give thy strength to thy servant, and save the son of thine handmaid. Shew me a token for good, that they which hate me may see it and be ashamed, because thou, Lord, hast healed me and comforted me. Based on the Word of God, Father show mercy unto me against every sin I have committed that has not allowed me to connect with my right spouse.

➤ *"Let thine ear now be attentive, and thine eyes open, that thou mayest hear the prayer of thy servant, which I pray before thee now, day and night, for the children of Israel, thy servants, and confess the sins of the children of Israel, which we have committed against thee: both I and my father's house have sinned.*" Father, in the name of Jesus Christ, I repent of every sin I have committed and the sins of my parents. Have mercy on us and deliver us from every stronghold. I receive cleansing for every abomination committed by me or my parents (Psalm 86:15-17).

➤ Father, in the name of Jesus Christ, I thank you as I engage in this spiritual warfare prayer that you will be a wall of fire as a covering for me against the kingdom of darkness. Send your mighty host of armies in heaven to fight every battle, and victory is mine (Psalm 103:20).

➤ As for thee also, by the blood of thy covenant, I have sent forth thy prisoners out of the pit, wherein is no water. Because of the blood of the Covenant, I break every effect of a curse or generational curses working against my martial destiny. With the help of the Lord, I decree my release from every generational curse, divination, enchantment spell, or evil agreement affecting my life. (Declare the curses or generational curses broken right now).

- Blood of Jesus, blot my name out of the evil register of "thou shalt not marry" or "divorce" in the name of Jesus. BE BLOTTED OUT NOW BY THE BLOOD OF JESUS CHRIST.

- DO A BLOOD BATH FOR 7 DAYS IF YOU NORMALLY WAKE UP TO SEE STRANGE MARKS IN YOUR BODY. Say the blood of Jesus Christ will destroy the effect of unprofitable marks standing as a limitation on my martial destiny.

- *"Now the Lord had said unto Abram, get thee out of thy country, and from thy kindred, and from thy father's house, unto a land that I will shew thee; and I will make of thee a great nation, and I will bless thee, and make thy name great; and thou shalt be a blessing; and I will bless them that bless thee, and curse him that curses thee; and in thee shall all families of the earth be blessed."* Say, "I come out from under the evil foundation of my mother's and father's house in the name of Jesus Christ" (mention your name). say it 7x times. (Genesis 12:1-2).

➤ Everything representing me on the demonic altars stopping my marital breakthrough catches fire, and I stop the operation of darkness speaking against my marital destiny from the evil altar.

➤ *"Lift up your heads, O ye gates; even lift them up, ye everlasting doors, and the King of glory shall come in. Who is this King of Glory? The Lord of hosts, he is the King of glory."* By the spoken word of God, I made a command: Let every ancient gate and everlasting door shut against my marital breakthrough be forced open right now in Jesus' name. Command the door to be opened, and your marital partner will locate you. (Psalm 24:9:10).

➤ *"So she took off her widow's garments, covered herself with a veil and wrapped herself, and sat in an open place which was on the way to Timnah; for she saw that Shelah was grown, and she was not given to him as a wife"* (Genesis 38:14). Say, In the name of Jesus Christ, I command the fire from heaven to locate any spiritual veil placed upon me to blindfold the right spouse from coming to me. Say, "Holy Ghost Fire, consume every veil x7."

➤ ***"Go into the village opposite you, where as you enter you will find a colt tied, on which no one has ever sat. Loose it and bring it here."*** Father, as you command the donkey to be untied, so I command my right husband or wife to be to locate me in Jesus' name. (Luke 19:30)

Chapter

7

PRAYERS FOR THE UNSAVED

7
Prayer for the Unsaved

The Bible says in 1 Timothy 2:1-2

"I exhort therefore, that, first of all, supplications, prayers, intercessions, and giving of thanks, be made for all men; For kings, and for all that are in authority; that we may lead a quiet and peaceable life in all godliness and honesty."

We have heard how many men, women, and children are suffering from drug addiction, gun violence, armed robbery, and engaging in errors. If we don't pray for our new converts and our family members, we may not have a quiet and peaceful life in our homes, cities, or nation.

Samson's parents did not intercede for their son, and that is why he walked in error. Hannah made a vow to God and dedicated her unborn child to Him. Because of her prayer of faith, Samuel fulfilled his destiny.

Testimony

I was told to pray for a boy who used a knife to fight people, stole, and also drank. One day, I took his name to my prayer altar and invoked the power of God upon his name and his picture. I told the boy to get anointing oil, and I prayed that the Spirit of God would enter the oil for his deliverance. Then, I instructed him to rub it on his body. After the prayer, I saw the boy in my dream sitting on a bed with a man sitting beside him. I asked the boy what he was doing there, and he said, "This is the man who detained him." Also, the boy said his parents said he was stealing, but he said it was not that he intended to steal but that there is a spirit that comes upon him to misbehave. No one knows how the evil spirit enters the lives of our new converts, but the power of prayer and erecting an altar before them will overturn every situation and give them hope.

"Then Noah built an altar to the Lord, and took of every clean animal and of every clean bird, and offered burnt offerings on the altar. And the Lord smelled a soothing aroma. Then the Lord said in His heart, "I will never again curse the ground for man's sake, although the imagination of man's heart is evil from his youth; nor will I again destroy every living thing as I have done. "While the earth remains, Seedtime and harvest, Cold and heat, Winter and summer, and day and night Shall not cease". Gen.8:20-22.

Prayer alone is not enough when you want your new converts or family members to change their evil ways to God's way. Noah built an altar to God, and immediately God smelled the aroma. God said, "I will not again curse the ground anymore for man's sake." Sow a sacrificial seed towards the person you believing God for his or her turnaround.

"But this is a people robbed and plundered; all of them are snared in holes, and they are hidden in prison houses; they are for prey, and no one delivers; for plunder, and no one says, "Restore!" (Isaiah 42:22).

Prayer Points for the Unsaved

Sing this song: "Holy Ghost, arise in your power, power to deliver, power to save, power to deliver, power to set us free, Holy Ghost, arise in your power.

1. Father, in the name of Jesus Christ, I praise you with all of my being. You are the rock of my salvation, the righteous God, the merciful God, my defender, my redeemer, and the compassionate God. I thank you for your loving kindness towards all the unsaved souls.

2. Father, in the greatness of your power, turn to them, oh God of our salvation, and cause thine anger to cease toward the unsaved soul. Revive them and let them be revived.

3. Father, in the name of Jesus Christ, I thank you for turning around our unsaved soul and for restoring unto them your presence for having mercy upon their dwelling place. For out of their mouths shall proceed thanksgiving. Jer. 30:17.

4. Father, in the name of Jesus, by the power of the Holy Ghost, unloose every band of wickedness, programmed to stop the unsaved souls from being established in the Lord and in faith: Speak in tongues for their release.

5. Undo every heavy burden and let the glory of God be upon the unsaved souls.

6. I prophesy the unsaved in our family and around us are released from every oppression, and every yoke stopping their release is broken right now in Jesus' name. (Romains 26:27).

7. As the mountains surround Jerusalem, so the Lord will surround all our new converts. Say father, in the name of Jesus Christ, we decree all the unsaved souls will hear the voice of God and will follow you to the end. O Lord, give them eternal life, and they shall never perish; nor shall any man pluck them out of God's hand. (John 10:27-28).

8. I pray for a new heart, and a new spirit will God put in you; he will take away the stone heart from your flesh, and I will give you a heart of flesh. The Lord will guide you and take you to the place where you will fulfill your destiny and serve God all the days of your life, causing you to walk in His status. (Ezekiel 36:26-27).

9. He answered and said, "Whether he be a sinner or not, I know not; one thing I know is that, whereas I was blind, now I see."

10. Say, "Father, in the name of Jesus Christ, I thank you for opening the spiritual eyes of the unsaved souls, thereby establishing them in the Lord and taking them to their place of worship, where the powers of the wicked will no longer locate them in Jesus' name."

Thank you for answering prayer (John 9:27).

Chapter

8

DAILY CONFESSION

8

Daily Confession

"You will also declare a thing, and it will be established for you; So, light will shine on your ways." Proverb 22:28

"Death and life are in the power of the tongue: and they that love it shall eat the fruit thereof." Proverbs 18:12

- ➢ I am Helped.

- ➢ I am rich and favored.

- ➢ I live in good health.

- ➢ I have the Holy Ghost in me.

- ➢ I have the righteousness of God in me.

- ➢ I have a new heart and a new spirit.

- ➢ I will not die before my time but live to fulfill my destiny on this earth.

- I shall not build for another to inhabit; I shall not plant for another to eat. I will long enjoy the work of my hands.

- The gates of my destiny shall continually be open for greatness.

- The blood of Jesus cancels every negative word that is working against my destiny, and I decree blessings to be following me.

- Every evil covenant with death programmed against my life—marriage, marital destiny, finances, or every area of my life—be destroyed by fire, and I decree life in the journey of my life.

- The Lord will make me an everlasting excellence and a joy for many generations.

- I decree that kindness and God's favor will follow me all the days of my life.

- I live in good health, and no sickness will come near me.

- No arrow that flies by day or terror by night will come near my dwelling place.

- There shall no evil befall me, nor shall any plague come nigh my dwelling place, for the Lord will give his angels charge over me to keep me in all my ways.

- The Lord will cause my enemies who rise up against my family to be smitten before our faces; they shall come out against us one way and flee before us seven ways.

- The little blessings in my hands will become a thousand, and the Lord will hasten it in his time.

- I shall win souls for God's kingdom and I will make Heaven.

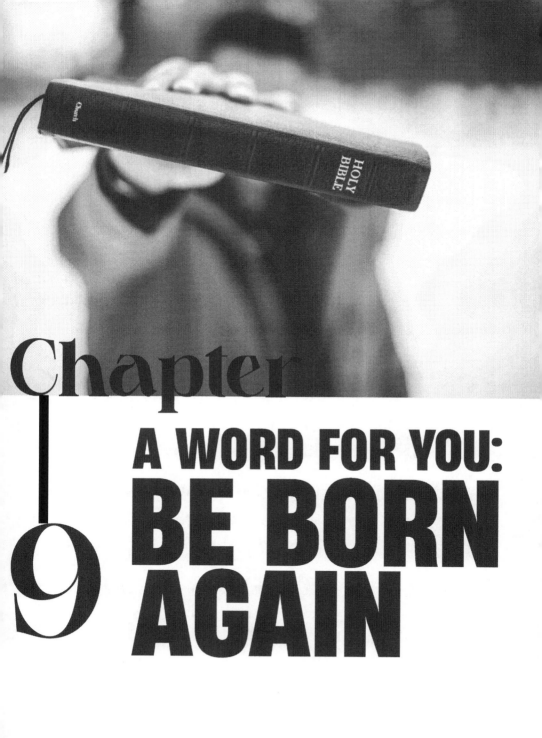

Chapter

9

A WORD FOR YOU:
BE BORN AGAIN

9
A Word for You:
Be Born Again

"Therefore, if any man be in Christ, he is a new creature: old things are passed away; behold, all things are become new." 2 Cor. 5:14.

Do you know that the day you were born is when you start a journey? This journey will either lead you to hell or heaven. If you are rich and eternity is far from you, then your existence is not worth living.

Death is an appointment that everyone must face; you cannot negotiate it. So, drop every wrong or sin that easily befalls you and start right now to do God's will.

Good things will come to you when you are born again.

Acquaint now thyself with him, and be at peace: thereby good shall come unto thee.

"If you return to the Almighty, you will be built up; He will remove iniquity far from your tents.

Then you will lay your gold in the dust, and the gold of Ophir among the stones of the brooks.

Yes, the Almighty will be your gold and your precious silver; for then you will have your delight in the Almighty and lift up your face to God." (Job 22:23-26)

"For the kingdom of God is not meat and drink; but righteousness, and peace, and joy in the Holy Ghost. For he that in these things serveth Christ is acceptable to God, and approved of men." (Romans 14:17-20)

The most important thing in the journey of your life is to accept the Lord Jesus as your savior and be truly born again. *(Jesus answered and said unto him, Verily, verily, I say unto thee, except a man be born again, he cannot see the kingdom of God).* (John 3:3)

To be born again means you are no longer engaged in the old sins you normally craved when you were still in the world.

"Now the works of the flesh are manifest, which are these: adultery, fornication, uncleanness, lasciviousness, idolatry, witchcraft, hatred, variance, emulations, wrath, strife, seditions, heresies, envyings, murders, drunkenness, reveling, and such like; of the which I tell you before, as I have also told you in time past, that they which do such things shall not inherit the kingdom of God." (Galatians 5:19-21)

For they that are after the flesh do mind the things of the flesh, but they that are after the Spirit the things of the Spirit. (Romans:8-5).

You cannot put a new garment over an old one. If you do such a thing, you cannot be comfortable. Moreso, to be able to overcome the kingdom of darkness, you need to be empowered by the Holy Ghost and live a righteous life.

Heaven and hell are real. You know life is a journey, so every time you sin, the enemy will deter you from fulfilling your destiny. When you are truly born again, you will enjoy God's goodness, favor, protection, and divine fulfillment, and you will make heaven your home.

Chapter

10

HOW TO START YOUR NEW LIFE WITH JESUS CHRIST

How to Start Your New Life with Jesus Christ

a) Confess that Jesus is Lord *(1 John 5:5)*.

b) Study and meditate on God's word daily *(Joshua 1:8)*.

c) Prayer without ceasing *(1 Thessalonians 5:17)*.

d) Fasting is very important *(Mark 9:29)*.

e) Go to church and be planted in the house of God *(Psalm 92:13)*.

f) Go make disciples of all nations. *(Mathew 28:19)*

MAKE THESE CONFESSIONS IF YOU ARE NOT BORN AGAIN.

Father, in the name of Jesus, I acknowledge you as my Lord and Savior, Jesus Christ, and I denounce Satan and all his evil works in my life. I know that I have sinned against you, and I ask for forgiveness. Cleanse me and give me a new heart and a new spirit. Let the power of the Holy Spirit overshadow my life. Let me hear your voice to guide me in the right way of righteousness, so that my ways will please you till eternity. Thank you for answering my prayer.

Made in the USA
Columbia, SC
19 June 2024

37002027R00065